For my grandmother, who saw faeries in the garden.

Para mi abuela, quien vio hadas en el jardín.

Believe the Wee Frog
La Pequeña Rana

Written and Illustrated by Sarah Wolfe

Escrito e ilustrado por Sarah Wolfe

Publisher's Cataloging-in-Publication
(Provided by Quality Books, Inc.)

Wolfe, Sarah.
  Believe the wee frog/ author & illustrator, Sarah
Wolfe. —1st ed.
    p. cm
    SUMMARY: Do fantasy creatures really exist? Keep your
eyes open and trust what you see!
    LCCN 2001093520
    ISBN 0-9701107-2-3

1. Self-confidence--Juvenile fiction. 2. Fairies--
Juvenile fiction. 3. Animals, Mythical--Juvenile
Fiction. [1.Self-confidence--Fiction. 2. Fairies--
Fiction. 3. Animals, Mythical--Fiction. 4. Stories in
rhyme.] I. Title.

PZ8.3.W8428Be 2001   [E]
            QB101-700966

Spanish translation by Creative Marketing of Green Bay, LLC

The illustration on page 5 was inspired by a
Carol and David Hughes photograph, © 1983, which appeared on the
cover of National Geographic magazine, Vol. 163, No. 1, January 1983.

This book is printed with soy inks on recycled paper.
Printed and manufactured in the United States of America
10 9 8 7 6 5 4 3 2 1

first edition

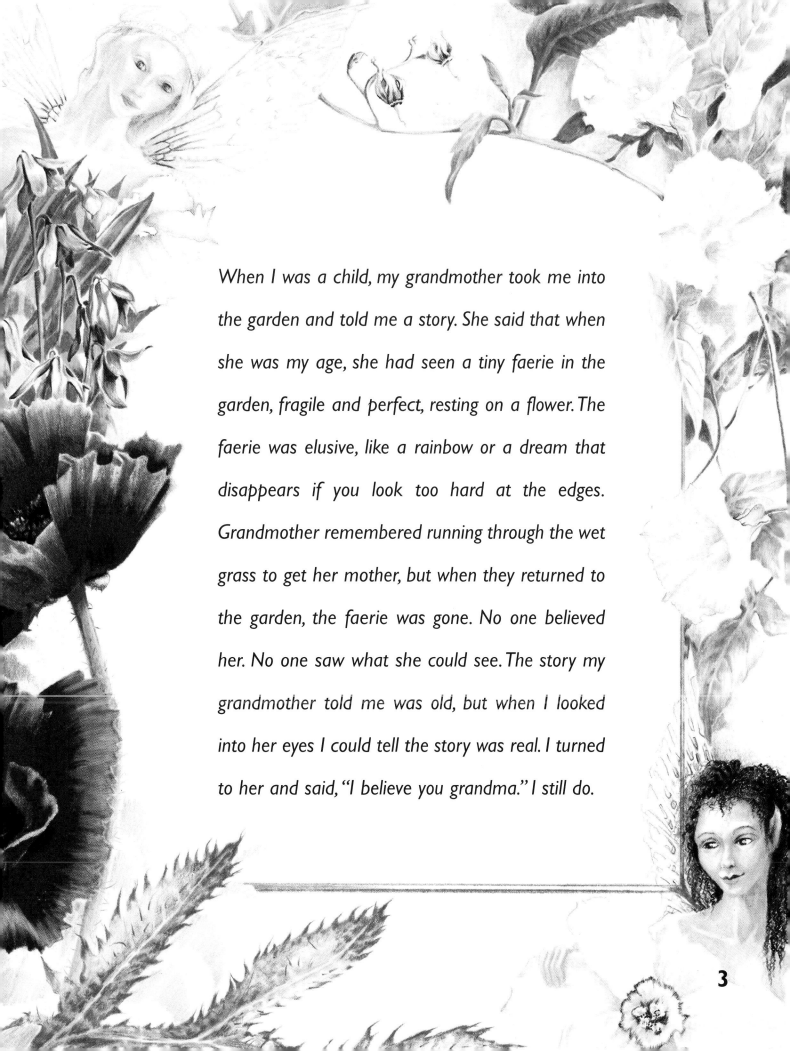

When I was a child, my grandmother took me into the garden and told me a story. She said that when she was my age, she had seen a tiny faerie in the garden, fragile and perfect, resting on a flower. The faerie was elusive, like a rainbow or a dream that disappears if you look too hard at the edges. Grandmother remembered running through the wet grass to get her mother, but when they returned to the garden, the faerie was gone. No one believed her. No one saw what she could see. The story my grandmother told me was old, but when I looked into her eyes I could tell the story was real. I turned to her and said, "I believe you grandma." I still do.

3

There is a wee frog

Not many have seen;

It sits in the mist

On an island of green.

But the island is really

The head of a Jed,

Who has no hair there

So grows plants there

instead!

And Jed's jungle

needs sunlight

To stay green and happy

So...

The Jed suns his head

On the brow

of a Zappy!

Who...

Swims in the

Tears of the

Bleary-eyed Blats

Who cries when it flies

To keep out the gnats

That swarm

     when it's warm

In the breath

     of some bats.

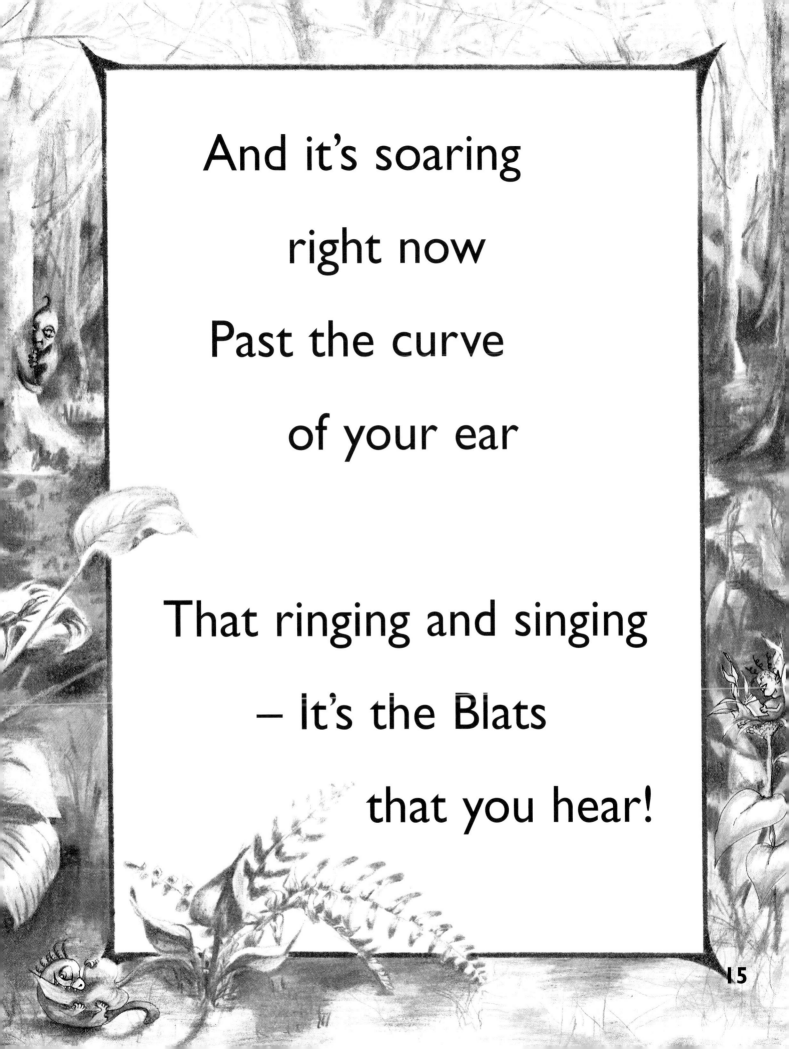

And it's soaring

right now

Past the curve

of your ear

That ringing and singing

– It's the Blats

that you hear!

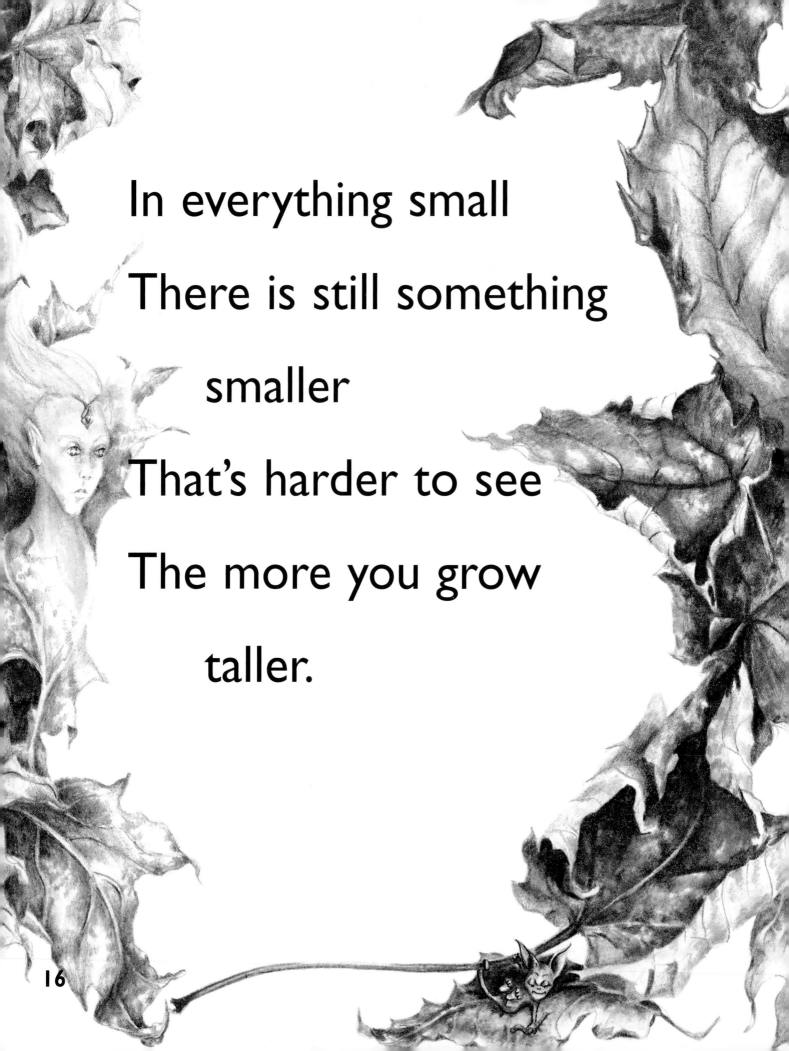

In everything small

There is still something

smaller

That's harder to see

The more you grow

taller.

So keep your eyes open

And believe what you see

Just because no one noticed

Doesn't mean it can't be!

The End

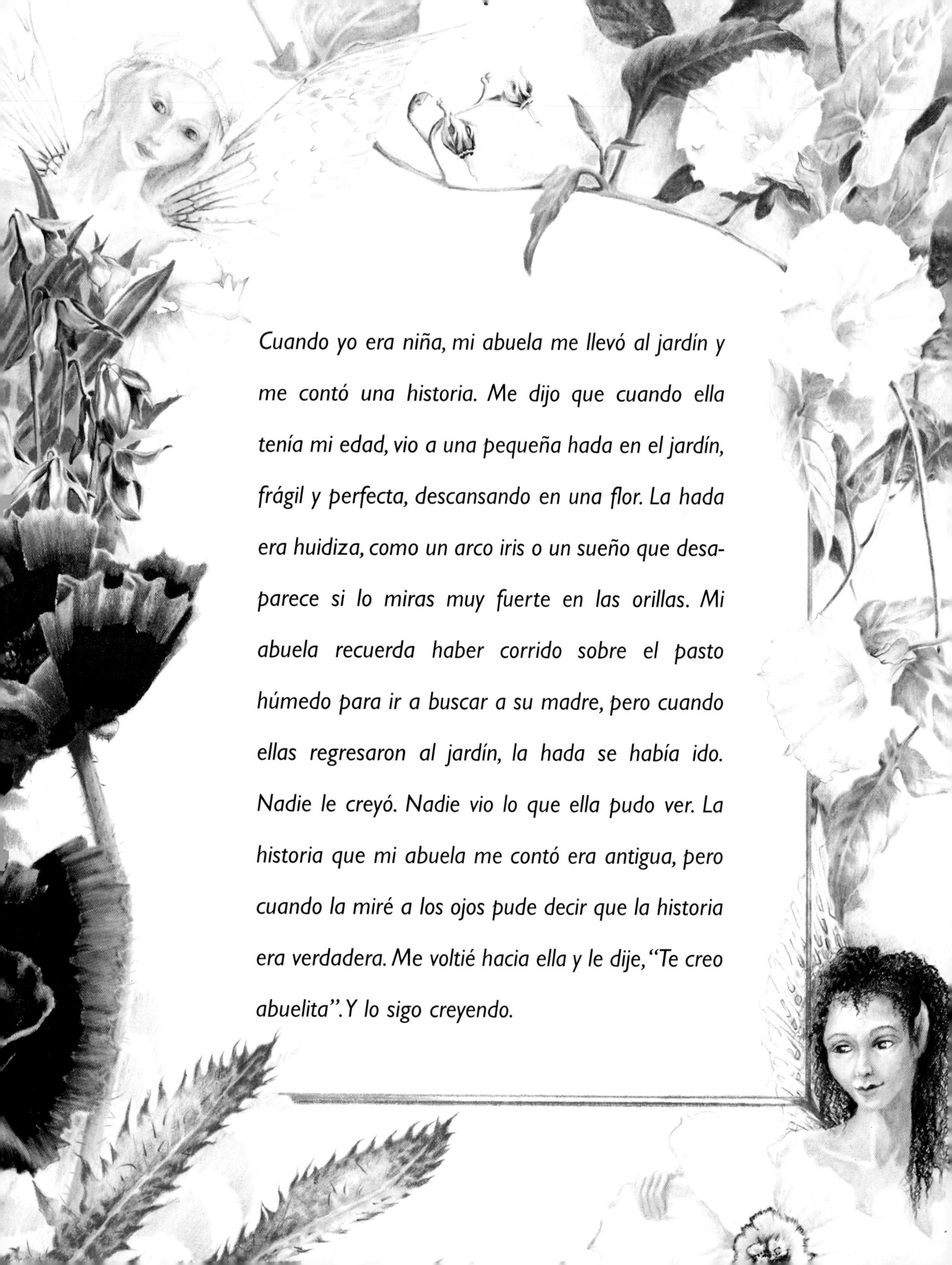

Cuando yo era niña, mi abuela me llevó al jardín y me contó una historia. Me dijo que cuando ella tenía mi edad, vio a una pequeña hada en el jardín, frágil y perfecta, descansando en una flor. La hada era huidiza, como un arco iris o un sueño que desaparece si lo miras muy fuerte en las orillas. Mi abuela recuerda haber corrido sobre el pasto húmedo para ir a buscar a su madre, pero cuando ellas regresaron al jardín, la hada se había ido. Nadie le creyó. Nadie vio lo que ella pudo ver. La historia que mi abuela me contó era antigua, pero cuando la miré a los ojos pude decir que la historia era verdadera. Me voltié hacia ella y le dije, "Te creo abuelita". Y lo sigo creyendo.

Hay una pequeña rana

Que nadie ha visto;

Se sienta en la neblina

Sobre una verde isla.

Pero la isla es en

realidad

La cabeza de un Jed,

Quien no tiene cabello

Y en su lugar le crecen

plantas

La isla de Jed necesita

luz del sol

Para permanecer verde

y feliz

Por lo tanto...

El Jed asolea su cabeza

Bajo la frente de un Zappy

Quien...

Nada en las

Lágrimas de los

Ojos exhaustos de Blats

Quien llora cuando vuela

para alejar al jején

que hormiguea cuando

el clima es cálido

en el aliento de algunos

murciélagos

12

Y ahora está

remontando el vuelo

Pasa la curva de tu oreja

Que zumbando y

cantando

Es el Blats

que escuchas

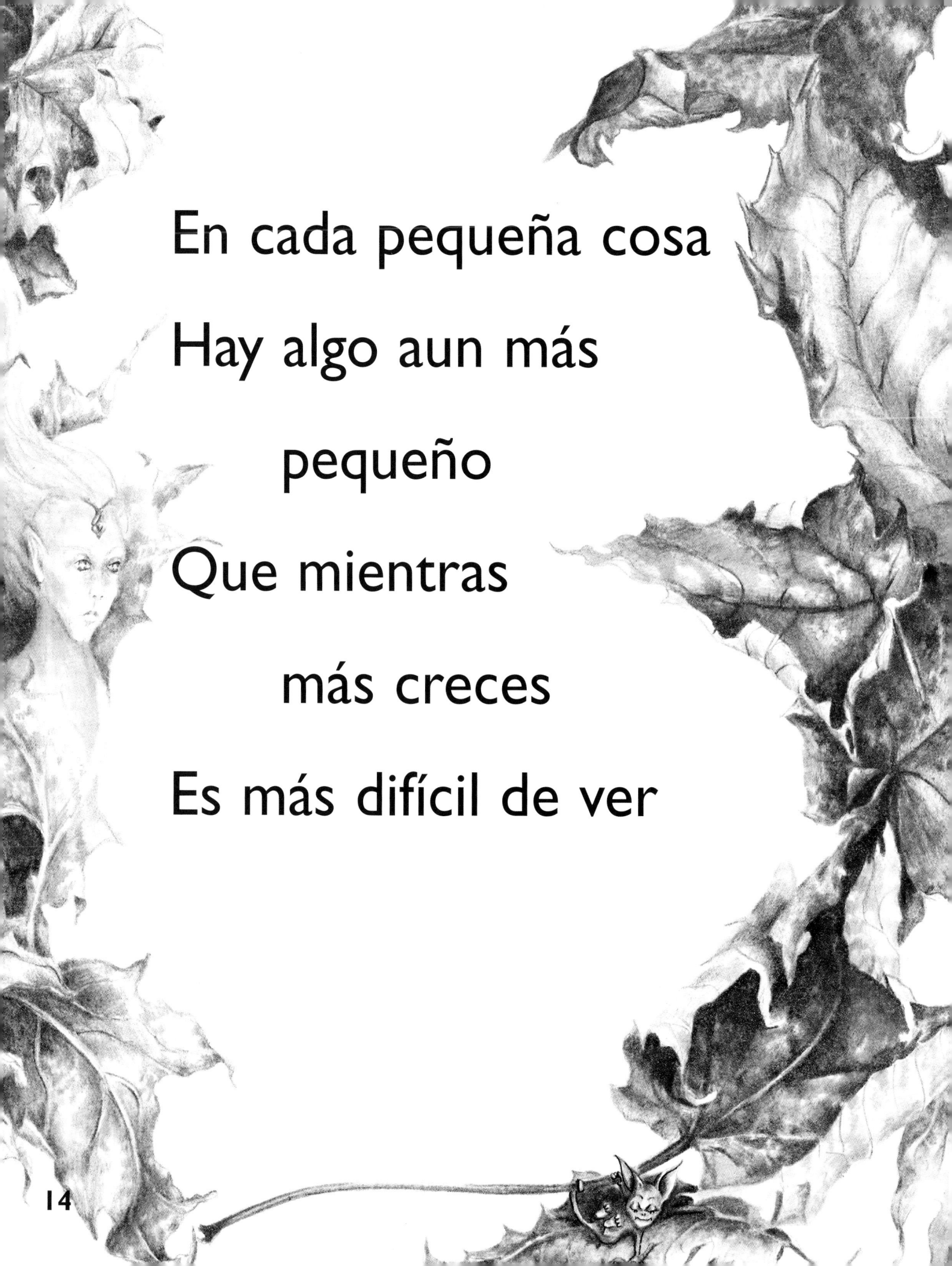

En cada pequeña cosa

Hay algo aun más

pequeño

Que mientras

más creces

Es más difícil de ver

Así que manten tus ojos

abiertos

Y cree lo que ves

Solo porque nadie

lo notó

No significa que no

pueda existir

El Final